SMILING SERVICE
A guide to etiquette and professionalism in the food industry.

Roxanne Easley

Atlanta, GA

Copyright ©2022 by Roxanne Easley
All rights reserved.

No portion of this book may be reproduced in any form without written permission from the publisher or author, except as permitted by U.S. copyright law.

This publication is designed to provide accurate and authoritative information in regard to the subject matter covered. It is sold with the understanding that neither the author nor the publisher is engaged in rendering legal, investment, accounting or other professional services. While the publisher and author have used their best efforts in preparing this book, they make no representations or warranties with respect to the accuracy or completeness of the contents of this book and specifically disclaim any implied warranties of merchantability or fitness for a particular purpose. No warranty may be created or extended by sales representatives or written sales materials. The advice and strategies contained herein may not be suitable for your situation. You should consult with a professional when appropriate. Neither the publisher nor the author shall be liable for any loss of profit or any other commercial damages, including but not limited to special, incidental, consequential, personal, or other damages.

Published with assistance from Expected End Entertainment:
ExpectedEndEntertainment@gmail.com
Address book and workshop inquiries to:
SmilingServiceTraining@gmail.com
Book Cover Photo by Ya Momz House Inc.
Hair: Fahrenheit the Evolution
Make up: Chekesha Lynn
Nails: Mary Gangliero
ISBN: 9781737146247

ACKNOWLEDGEMENTS

I am so grateful to share the knowledge I have gained over the years in the service and food industry. I would like to give a special thank you to my daughter, Tiara. I would not be where I am and wouldn't have pushed so hard had it not been for you! I love you and thank you for your support and patience in sharing me with the world. I would like to thank my parents, my extended family and loved ones for your continued encouragement.

To my Roxanne's Catering Family, I thank you! You have shown the world how the teachings of this book are put into action. You set the standard and it makes everyone know...it works! I appreciate each and every one of you from the beginning to the present. You've shown dedication to this mission. Thank you, Chuck Brown, for your direction and leadership during this process. I cannot thank you enough. Thank you to Emmai Alaquiva for capturing me in a light I hadn't seen before.

To those who read and follow this workbook... I thank YOU! Put into action the guidelines inside these pages and watch the growth of your company.

FOR WORKSHOPS
Call: 412.606.5938
or
Email:
SmilingServiceTraining@gmail.com

CONTENTS

	Introduction	i
1	Perception	1
2	The Importance of Time	13
3	Meet and Greet	23
4	DOs and DON'Ts	31
5	Service with a Smile	39
6	Social Media Conduct	47
7	Be Uniquely YOU!	59
8	BONUS CHAPTER	65
9	About the Author	77

INTRODUCTION

My name is Roxanne Easley, owner of Roxanne's Catering, Easley Event Staffing, and Smiling Service. I have been an entrepreneur for 17 years and working in the food/service industry for over 25 years.

Roxanne's Catering is known in the Pittsburgh area for quality food but also for exceptional service. Our motto is, "You can have a great product, but people will not work with you if you have horrible service. A client can forgive a mistake, but that's only if you provide exceptional service!" My belief is that service is more important than the product you are providing. The reason behind that logic is your product can change and improve over time, but your service is what draws the customer to you and keeps them. We pride our company on excellent service and now I am ready to teach you how to instill our motto into your business. I am presenting a series of trainings to help you and your staff earn positive feedback on reviews for google, yelp and social media outlets. With this series, our ultimate goal is to increase your sales. We all know service is key to a successful company. Just look at "Chick-fil-A"!

CHAPTER 1
PERCEPTION

We are all taught 1st impressions are everything. Walking into an office, event, or restaurant the first person you see someone sets the tone for what your experience will be.

First impressions include your greeting and your demeanor. Your posture can even give a person a negative or positive vibe. When you travel, you always SEE first. By the time you approach the first person you see, you have already formulated an impression.

The key is learning to manage the art of a lasting first impression. To do so you must observe the room. You must learn to adjust to the individuals you are serving. I call this research before arrival. With this skill you are also formulating an idea of whom you are meeting. Most may call this code switching. I call it knowing your audience. Now, learning to manage the art of 1st impressions is important because you don't get a second chance to make that 1st impression. If you don't manage correctly, you could miss out on potential opportunities.

The primary effect is the tendency for facts, impressions, or items that are presented to be learned or remembered later. This effect can occur during social interactions. It can result in the first impression bias, in which the first information gained about a person has an influence on later impressions and evaluations of that person.

For example, when you receive a call regarding services, your tone in your voice is the first impression. Speak with volume and confidence, and make sure you are knowledgeable about your subject matter. At this time, you are engaging with your client and inviting them into a conversation where they feel they are receiving personal attention. Always make sure your clients feel they are your #1 priority. Once you have had a conversation, it may be time to meet in person. This is where you need to be a showstopper! You want to wow them on sight. Never allow anyone to have a negative impression of you at first sight. With that being said, we've always been taught that eye contact and a strong handshake make a difference. And YES, they do. Let's put the skills we've learned as children to good use to make a 1st impression.

It takes 20 seconds for someone to formulate an opinion of who you are to them. Just that easy, a person can decide if they want to continue to do business with you. In the case of service, you want your 1st impression to have a positive impact on your business. You may decide you may not want to make a great 1st impression and continue to do business as usual. You, in fact, may do that! My question is why not try the Smiling Service way and watch your income grow just from making an awesome 1st impression?

Take a look at ways to make a great 1st impression. Study them and trust that they will begin to change within yourself, your staff, and the response from your clients.

MAKING A GREAT 1st IMPRESSION:

Dress for the occasion: Whether it's an interview, an informal or formal meeting, or an event, you must ensure you put your best foot forward. Give thought to the environment you will be in and dress appropriately for the occasion. The way you look can also help you feel good about yourself! Dressing for the occasion could mean casual, business casual, or business attire. This is appropriate for a meeting but also can be appropriate for an event. It is good to invest in your company, and branding is important. Make yourself and your company known wherever and whenever you are seen. Your staff should always be in proper uniform. You need to set the example for this to take effect. How you show up sets the tone for how your staff will follow. Make proper dress mandatory for your company and don't accept anything less. Expectations for your company should be a standard.

Dressing for the occasion also means making sure your clothing is clean and presentable. If you wear a uniform and you are in the public, make sure you are clean and wrinkle free. Your presence is an example of the company you represent. Your nails and haircare are also included as a 1st impression. It is the first image someone sees when encountering you. When someone shakes your hand with dirty hands or nails, how does that make you feel?

Imagine seeing this with someone who handles your food product. These minor improvements can change the trajectory of how potential clients see you and your staff members.

Be polite no matter the circumstance: In any case of meeting someone, there is no reason to be rude. In the service industry, you will encounter some people who will not always show you that same respect. The best method to use is, "Kill 'em with kindness!" I'm sure you have heard that term before. Understand this works in any case. Remember, you do not have to continue to put yourself in an uncomfortable situation. You can be the best version of yourself and speak with compassion. Oftentimes, you can prevent a verbal altercation by responding in a soft tone. This allows the situation to deescalate and helps for understanding. The way you communicate with your client, or your employees, sets the tone for building relationships. This can also be represented in email conversations. I'm sure you have had instances where a text message has been misconstrued. It will oftentimes happen during emails as well. Making a phone call can often fix this. In any instance, being polite is the key! When it becomes difficult to respond to someone who is being blatantly disgruntled, it is acceptable to ask them if you could work toward a resolution so both parties are satisfied. Allow them to suggest ways to resolve the issue. In most cases, it may be something as small as the client wanting to be acknowledged about what occurred. Allow your customer the opportunity to express their experience.

Lasting impression: When greeting someone, a formal handshake can go a long way. This is what I meant by those skills we learned as a child. Making a friendly and positive entrance will make a lasting impression. Eye contact is also important. When first meeting someone, social anxiety can be challenging. Do your best when engaging to remain present in the conversation, listening and making sure the person understands their words are important to you. Use your common sense and experiences to present the best version of yourself. There will be times you may get nervous and fumble your words, and that's okay. Just keep smiling. It's a part of a lasting impression. Correct yourself and continue to engage in conversation with your clients and/or employees. Be your humanly self that may make a humanly mistake at times. Most people want to see you authentic and not superficial. Engaging in conversations can involve a personal story or experience that your consumer can relate to. Interacting with your employees can help them feel that they can connect with you professionally and socially. It builds trust. Keep your conversations on a positive note, even in a negative situation. Your goal is to allow someone to see the bright side of a circumstance. It is easier to show someone negativity because of the world we live in today. Give them a positive experience every time they are in your presence.

Smiling is KEY: Your smile is inviting and approachable. Wherever you are and whatever the circumstance, a genuine smile is going to be your best accessory. Hence the title, "Smiling Service Training". The first thing a client should see as you are approaching is how happy you are to greet them. A smile can oftentimes calm a disgruntled person. How can you be angry at someone that is smiling at you and ready to help? Guess what? You can even tell someone is smiling through a mask. Smiling changes the mood and the atmosphere. It shows character and sets a peaceful nonverbal tone. In a high stress atmosphere, smiling can decrease the tension that may build. Showing an act of kindness can help. Your mood will be elevated, and smiling is known to cause relaxation within your body. Smiling inspires confidence when engaging others. Interaction with another person will be infectious when smiling, even in a professional environment. Smiling can ensure trust and compassion for one's needs. When you approach someone who is smiling at you, your natural reaction is to smile in return. Smiling at someone can produce positivity during your initial contact, which in return can set the tone for your meeting.

- During our training services we give examples of 1st impressions. We practice how to make a 1st impression and improve on our skills to create lasting impressions.

NOTES

NOTES

ROXANNE EASLEY

CHAPTER 2
THE IMPORTANCE OF TIME

Time management is the process of planning and exercising conscious control of time spent on specific activities, especially to increase effectiveness, efficiency and productivity.

In the service industry, time management includes your personal time and consideration of your client. Respecting someone's time makes a difference on how you are defined as a business owner. Prioritizing your daily tasks is most important to make sure you have adequate time to complete every project. Managing your time will increase the quality of your work because you are not rushing to complete a deadline. Rather, you set the appropriate time to complete each project with the necessary work required.

Have you heard the term, "Work smarter, not harder"? This stands true in every aspect of your life. Time has everything to do with this statement. You can get more work done in less time, even when you are pressed for time. Time is valuable and time is money. Wasting time becomes a loss of income. If you have staff that arrives late every day, it slows productivity. If you, as the owner, don't value the importance of time, how will your clients or your staff respect time? Not valuing time management can negatively impact your company, whether you are a catering company or a restaurant. Time management also is key to improving your bottom line. It shows the importance of the person receiving your services. You are valuing their time, which makes them want to continue doing business with you.

Arriving, delivering, and showing up to a meeting on time are all important factors in managing one's time. Time management must be a priority to those around you.

Tracking your employees' time is also an important key to effective time management. Your team must understand the importance of time management. Arriving to a shift after your start time can create a ripple effect with your organization. Once one staff member creates a habit of poor time management skills, it can ripple through your entire team. Remember, your staff is looking to you to create the standard of consequences when someone does not adhere to the time that has been assigned to them. As a manager or owner of your establishment, your team arriving late is a reflection of your business as a whole. Opening a restaurant late will not show as a reflection on the individual, but on the team as a whole. If a staff member or members consistently violate the protocol of time, you must reprimand them. You can offer a grace period for your team, approximately five minutes is fair, but if a team member is consistently violating you must take a firm stand to protect your business.

We are going to address the importance of managing your time, what happens when you do not manage time appropriately, and tools to help improve your time management.

Time Managing Scenarios:

1) You are booked for an event that begins at 6 p.m. Your guests will arrive at 5:30 p.m. but dinner will not be served until 6:30 p.m. What time is your arrival time?

_____
_____
_____

2) You are providing a breakfast for a staff meeting that begins at 8 a.m. The instructor wants the food ready and available for self-service by 7:30 a.m. What time do you arrive? What time do you wake up to start completing your order? Should you start the morning of or the night before?

_____
_____
_____

3) You are scheduled to speak at an engagement. You have never been to the venue before or met the hosts in person. Do you allow time to arrive and settle in or do you arrive just as the program is beginning?

_____
_____
_____

4) An event serving 200 guests is scheduled for Friday at 2 p.m. They will open the doors at 8 a.m. You have access to their onsite kitchen space. You also have to make sure the guest tables, food tables, and drink stations are all ready to go before the guests arrive. What time do you arrive?

_____
_____
_____

5) Your restaurant is set to open at 6 a.m. You must pre prep supplies. Your staff has to punch in, use the rest room, and get dressed in proper uniform. In addition, you have to make sure your coffee and tea are ready for servicing your customers. What time should your staff arrive?

_____
_____
_____

Answers:

1) Arrival time for an event where guests arrive at 5:30 p.m. should be 4:30 p.m. You need to allow at least one hour for a buffet set up. You do not want to be in the middle of setting up an event while guests are arriving. When your guests arrive, the only thing that should come out is hot food.

2) An early morning breakfast can be tricky. You should always start at least 3 hours before to make sure you are ready to go and arrive at the venue at least 45 minutes prior to start time. To do this, a night before prep would be ideal. Make sure you have your products ready and available for an immediate start. Check the location of the space on the GPS to know how much time you need to arrive and allow yourself time for set up (up to 45 min for a breakfast).

3) Always, **on every occasion**, allow time for arrival, parking, and greeting your hosts for any engagement. It's out of respect for the person who is asking for your presence and allows time to make sure you know what your environment will be.

4) This is very important!! Anytime a venue allows you access to an onsite kitchen for an event, USE IT! Pack your items so when they open the door at 8 a.m. you have arrived, unloaded and walk in the door ready to work! I can't stress this enough. An on-site kitchen is the best option in the catering business. This allows everything to be hot and fresh from the oven. It is also a plus if a venue will allow you the time to come in the night before to set up your space or even allow you to unload before the next morning.

5) You should always have a shift rotation. There should be someone who arrives at least 1 hour to 2 hours before opening. This person most likely will be the manager. They will set the assignments of the other staff members to ensure a proper opening time. We live in a hurry mentality society. Expect your customers to be ready in your restaurant or drive through when your lights are on.

TO BE EARLY IS TO BE ON TIME. TO BE ON TIME IS TO BE LATE. TO BE LATE IS TO SUFFER THE CONSEQUENCES.

NOTES

NOTES

CHAPTER 3
MEET AND GREET

This subject matter is very important to the success you are establishing in your business. Word of mouth and referrals are one and the same. The first impression is going to be the lasting impression that your client and their guests will use to create a review for your services. How you show up matters. As I stated in Chapter 1, your appearance matters.

Based on your phone conversations, your client has already formed their expectations of you and your services before you meet in person. In this case, it is now up to you to sell yourself and your product(s). Even if sales are not your business, you must be able to sell what you and your company do.

First, find out who your customer is, what they like, and what are their expectations. This is the research of your client we spoke about in the first chapter. The more information you obtain, the more you can build the relationship. By the time you meet your client in person, you should be greeting them with a smile on your face, ready to continue the work you started. Your work began with the first email, phone call, inbox, or in person. At that point, you are working to either gain their business or maintain it.

In that case, you are now showcasing your company and working to show your client how your company will best suit their needs. You must convince your client that you set your business apart from the competition in your industry. Show them why they should choose your restaurant or catering company over another one. Don't allow cost to be the deciding factor for your client. If you set your standards above the competition, your client will choose quality over quantity.

How will you do this?

I will reiterate... how you show up is important.

When you are starting in the service industry of catering or any other service organization, you may not have a lot of money. That's okay! Look at every meeting as a professional environment. How would you show up for an interview? As entrepreneurs, we often say we are our own bosses, but in actuality our bosses change daily. Your client is now your boss for the day, and you are working to please them for an opportunity in the future. With that being said, at a very low cost, a pair of black slacks, scrub pants, or chef pants with a plain shirt would suffice. Do not, I repeat do not, show up as a professional in a pair of lounge pants or leggings. The way you show up today will set the tone for tomorrow.

Invest in yourself and invest in your business. That could mean the Goodwill, Walmart, or any other low-priced locations to provide yourself with something that makes you look professional. People will often receive you based on your appearance.

When you arrive at an event, immediately greet your client. Make eye contact, a firm handshake, and introduce yourself with confidence. Reassure them they are in good hands. Check out your surroundings and get ready to do the work!

If you are a restaurant owner, your meet and greet happens more often. You will meet new guests by the minute or by the hour. This circles back to the first impression, greet your guests with a smile, welcoming tone, and the courtesy of providing the best service they will experience by walking into your establishment. Your goal is to increase revenue by having returning customers. Service is key! Your greeting will set the beginning of their experience. The food will have to do the rest!

MEETING YOUR CLIENT:

• Always present yourself with a smile and let them know they are in good hands.

• Ask as many questions as you can to be as confident as you need to be to make their event wonderful.

• Go above and beyond to make sure your client doesn't have to lift a finger, hence the reason they hired a professional.

• If you cannot do what is being asked, reach out to someone you know! There are resources and help everywhere. Believe it or not, most other businesses would be happy to lead you in a direction of your success.

• Arrive early for your first meeting and going forward. You are building trust. This is a relationship. You must build trust and maintain it.

• Again, what you don't know… ASK!

• Research the event, the client, and get to know them before you meet them. You may be able to give a recommendations to enhance their event once you've done your research. I keep reiterating the importance of doing your research. It matters!

• Most importantly, do not promise what you cannot deliver. There is nothing like being promised a service and not receiving it. You will set yourself up for a negative review and reputation.

NOTES

SMILING SERVICE

NOTES

CHAPTER 4
DOS AND DON'TS

I called this section dos and don'ts because I've made a lot of mistakes in this industry over the years. Today, I can teach from those experiences to help people like you to avoid some pitfalls and to learn early how to set high standards for your business as a professional in the service industry. This guide is to help you create your own standards for your company and manage your expectations in order to increase your revenue.

I pride myself on service. I make mistakes just like anyone, but my clients trust me and know that I am going to do my very best to correct any mistake. Not only am I going to correct it, but I am also going to attempt to make up for my mistake. Understand this, even if you have someone working with you and *they* make the mistake, if it makes it to the client, it's now *your* mistake. You are your business. No matter what happens, everything that comes in with *your* name is always going to be on *you*. Let's do our best to maintain etiquette in doing so.

- When you are starting, you may have friends and family helping you. That is great! Make sure they are clear on what you expect from them when dealing with your clients and their guests. They follow your lead.

- If a guest allows you to stay at an event, DO NOT eat any food, sample any product, or touch anything that they purchased from you. It is not yours any longer; it belongs to them. Most times, you are being invited to the event for networking reasons. Take advantage of that. Stand near your product, but don't make the room look at you negatively for any reason.

- If your staff has been invited to stay, the same goes for them. Even if the client says, "Hey, eat. It's okay", still do not. Wait till the end of the evening, while cleaning up, if there are any leftovers and they do not want to take the food home at this point, you should be welcomed to a plate. It is distasteful to take back a product you made for someone they spent money on for their guests.

- If your friends and family are interested in an event you are catering, do not invite them as a guest for free. This is very important. You can start a word-of-mouth chain about how you are taking advantage of the benefits that come with being in the room.

- If you work with any organization and they have a celebrity guest, do not ask for an autograph! It is unprofessional. Guess who won't be invited back if that person felt uncomfortable.

- Make yourself available to your client. Choose working hours between 8 a.m. and 5 p.m. as a good start. This could mean phone calls, emails, and text messages. At the end of the day, be sure to check on and follow up with your clients. Let them know they are important to you.

- Restaurant employees... do not offer free food to your friends and family at the cost of the company. If you are giving away food, the company is losing money, and you will have less chance of a raise in the future. Our goal is to increase revenue, not decrease. Make known the consequences of the actions of giving away a product and how it will affect the company and individual as a whole.

- Connect with like-minded individuals that are in the same business as you. Build relationships with fellow companies. Don't make them competition; there is enough money for everyone. Make them business friends. It is good to bounce ideas off one another in order to see that everyone can be successful. Why not help each other build? You don't have to lose your uniqueness in the process!

SMILING SERVICE

NOTES

SMILING SERVICE

NOTES

ROXANNE EASLEY

CHAPTER 5
SERVICE WITH A SMILE

Service with a smile! This is the key to providing great service. In this business, you will come across circumstances that will be tough. There will be difficult times, and on rare occasions, difficult clients. I say this because it is true. There are times when you can do everything under the sun, and someone is not going to be satisfied. Know that you cannot please everyone. But you can try.

There can be a number of reasons why your customer is not satisfied. There are instances where a customer may have ordered a certain amount of food, but they have more guests arrive than anticipated. You may run out of an entrée or a dish that was a popular choice. Now you must pivot. You can reduce the portions you provide but could still run out completely.

A restaurant may run out of a popular item on their menu. This may cause a disgruntled client, who may threaten to tell their friends about their experience. Now you have to do your best to make them feel that the money spent was a priority to you. You can correct this by offering a refund of services, an item free in the future, or additional services in the future of their choosing. Now, this may not solve every issue that you may encounter with a customer, but it shows effort!

You could have gotten the contract instead a friend of someone who was on the planning committee. You could have received menu options and some of their guests are not pleased with the options. There are many unfortunate instances you will encounter, but keep smiling. The best response is to offer a solution. Make sure the solution you offer is feasible on your end as well. Sometimes during this journey, you may take a loss, but the referral you will receive from how you handled the situation is what will continue to build your clientele. In the end, you continue to increase your revenue.

Here are helpful phrases when you are faced with a dilemma:

"How can we help?"

"Let's make this work. What can we do to make your experience better?"

"Unfortunately, these are the options we have today. Is there anything we can do?"

"At the end of the event, we want you to have the best experience. How about we _____ instead of _____? With my experience, I believe this would be the best solution."

"It is our pleasure to serve you today. How may we help you?"

"Whatever you need, we will work to the best of our ability to make your event a success!"

Your goal is to make this look easy. On some occasions, you will have to make an impossible situation seem possible. Service with a smile is going to change the mindset of how your client looks at an outcome. They need to trust your judgment. You, too, need to trust your judgement! Be confident in your decisions.

Make your staff a part of the decision to correct an error. Your staff is the glue to scenarios that you may overlook. Teamwork makes the dream work! Providing your staff sufficient information about different scenarios will give them the confidence to be involved and the opportunity to help with conflict resolutions.

Not only are you providing service to your clients, but your staff also needs your service with a smile as well. How will you reward them to make them feel valued?

The saying, "A happy wife is a happy life", goes the same for your staff! A happy staff makes sure your company continues to be a success! You cannot be everywhere at all times; you must build trust with those who are on site day to day. Their comfortability is as important as the clients you serve. They should be rewarded for their efforts in making sure your customers choose to return. It takes time to build those relationships with your staff and your costumers. Once you gain that trust, you most likely have a client for eternity and a staff member that will ride with you till the wheels fall off.

NOTES

NOTES

CHAPTER 6
SOCIAL MEDIA CONDUCT

Social media presence is important in today's society. How you represent yourself to the world in the service industry can create a negative or positive experience for your potential customers. In the world we live in today, the first thing you do when someone mentions a business is go straight to Google. What they see may determine if they want to do business with you. In this chapter, we will examine the importance of your representation on social media platforms.

There are approximately 243.5 million Facebook users in the United States alone. That means you have millions of users that can see your Facebook content at any given time. Depending on how active you are, just remember eyes are on you! Now that you can create "reels", it opens your social media to the public. You never know how many people your content will reach.

Instagram is also a very highly used social media outlet. There are more than 161 million users in the United States alone. You have to think of all social media as free exposure for your business.

In the beginning stages of your business, you would most likely handle your own social media needs. As your business grows, you may elect to have a social media manager. This person would post statuses, pictures, and content representing your business. It is important that your social media manager knows who your target audience is and how you would like your business to be represented.

Social media allows for an online networking community. How you conduct yourself can represent the company. This also falls in line with first impressions. The research that a customer does before they get to you is most likely a social media search.

Addressing Social Media Content:

In the service industry, you'll find mixed opinions on how social media will affect your revenue. It is important to separate your personal and company's pages. Doing so will give you a bit of freedom to post personal content you would like to share. You can also make your personal page private and only visible to friends and family. Although, most people are not as private as you may think.

If your target audience is children, hospitals, or a non-profit organization that represents religion or youth, you should be careful about what you allow on your page.

For instance, someone may tag you in a post from a party you attended the night before, in which you were visibly intoxicated. How do you think that company may move forward with you in the future? Now, understand not all organizations take this into consideration. The question is, why take the chance?

If you saw your child's paediatrician on social media with a shot in one hand and the middle finger in the air, would you think differently of them?

If the answer is no, then you may be in the minority. Best believe there will be someone who will not like it and it could start a social media frenzy.

Be careful what you post on all your social media outlets including LinkedIn. Remember to look at it as if you were looking for a product or service. How would you react? You are a public figure now and at times you have to adjust accordingly.

Handling negative comments on social media:
As a caterer or a representative in the food industry, oftentimes if we make one mistake, we are splattered on social media. Ninety percent of the posts may be positive but that 10% would attack you and your company for a mistake. It's not fair, but it is the world we live in today.

How do you handle these instances gracefully? Most times, you can resolve an issue before it hits Facebook. In those cases that you were not able to resolve, and negativity hits the "Book", it can spiral. First off, do not be combative with every comment. This will only make the matter worse. Reach out to the client that originally booked your services and see if you can correct your mistake. If they have already received the product, the solution is to offer compensation or a discounted event if they would like to book in the future. Most times this will work. It's all about your approach. Remember in the beginning I said your service will determine how someone will react to your mistake. If you exhibit excellent service, oftentimes you can avoid a negative connotation about your business.

How you respond to comments concerning your company will be either a negative or a positively reflection on your character and that of your company. As an established company, it would be wise to allow your social media manager or influencer to handle those needs. In doing so, the responses will not have an emotional attachment. As a business owner, negative responses can occur because you are passionate about your establishment, which you should be, but it could cause professional suicide. If you are a new business, just take time and patience when it comes to dealing with negative outbursts on social media. In other words, be slow to respond so that you don't make the mistake of having a back and forth argument via the internet.

You can't prevent them all, but you can limit them.

In the rare instances that someone posts a picture or blast your mistake on social media, sometimes you can ignore it, and it will blow over.

In the case that it does not, it's time to do your research. See who the people are who are commenting. They may be someone who has used your services in the past. Reach out to them personally and ask if the situation can be diffused. If so, it's an easy fix. If not, your best bet is to let it blow over and learn from your mistake. We are human. Errors will happen! It's how you recover that matters the most. Minor mistakes can range from being late, making the wrong entrée, or not having enough food. You can also make the mistake of preparing a dish that is not to the liking of the client. It is important to know that you cannot please everyone, but most importantly you need to please the client that hired you. You need to please the customer that is paying their hard-earned money for your services. Emphasis on "Service!"

A consumer will also take their gripe to, "Yelp" or "Google". These are also outlets clients and customers can share their experiences with you and your company. You may read the comments and feel that this is not an accurate statement of what occurred. Remember, the consumer is making a statement from their experience not yours. You cannot argue that. The best way to respond is to first comment, "We apologize for your experience. Can we offer a gift card for a future visit and refund for the date of your service?" The goal is to work harder to prevent the negativity but also be aware of instances that may occur that you had no knowledge of. You cannot be at all places at the same time, even with cameras present. This is why proper service training for your staff is imperative. Not only will it reduce the amount of negative responses, but it will increase your bottom line.

How often do you see, "Chick-fil-A" as a subject of an internet post complaining about their order or service? Very rarely. That is because they uphold their staff to a standard that any mistake is resolved instantly. They make sure their team is considered a unit, not individuals. If one person makes a mistake, WE made the mistake, and they correct it with smiles and professionalism.

In the fast food or restaurant industry, these concepts apply. If you have a disgruntled customer, they will often take their gripe to social media outlets to be heard. Oftentimes consumers will take this route because their experience is that they were not handled with care from the service provider. As business owners, you may have an employee who may not have had a good day or isn't properly trained on how to handle a disgruntled customer. No worries, anyone can change! People need to feel valued. That applies to the consumer and the company providing the service. It is up to the management team to make sure the staff feels valued at what service they are providing and that will create a ripple effect of how that employee will treat the next customer they provide service to.

How you treat your team determines how they treat the consumer in return. To show your appreciation for your team, have an employee of the month, or offer lunch or breakfast. Something as simple as a card or recognition of their contribution goes a long way!

SMILING SERVICE

Your employees are just as important as your consumer.

NOTES

NOTES

CHAPTER 7
BE UNIQUELY YOU!

In the food industry, especially the catering industry, you will find yourself in a realm of many companies that may be a mirror image of your own. That's why creating a brand of your own company is so important.

You must discover what you want your image and your brand to represent for your company. You have to decide what makes you unique to all the other companies in your industry. The question becomes, "Why choose me?" You must answer this to understand how to establish yourself and where to focus your growth.

There are many tools in the food industry that can help you, just like "Smiling Service Training". You must decide which tools work best for you to express your creativity in everything you do.

"Pinterest" is a popular tool that can generate creativity when searching for ideas. You also can watch "TikTok" and other apps that will simulate ideas for you to develop your own brand.

In this industry, you have to respect your fellow and local catering companies. If you see them building a brand that you admire, it is okay to reach out to them. When reaching out, you may see something fantastic they have created. Ask for permission to use their design concept. If the company is out of state, you can still use their design as inspiration and make it unique to your company. You never want to mimic another company's brand, especially if you haven't thought of how to make it original. This can cause legal and copyright infringements that may catch up to you in the future. Honestly, why would you want to be someone else in the industry, when you can be uniquely you!

Pictures and videos speak volumes, especially being in the same city. Everyone uses social media as a free advertising platform. You do not want to be the company that follows behind another established company copying their business model. It looks unprofessional and can cause your company to be discredited.

If you admire the company that you follow, reach out to them. Maybe there is a mentoring opportunity in it for you. You may need to learn from that company instead of mimicking their every move. This will still help you build your own brand and also maintain respect. For example, celebrities and comedians will often support each other in film and production. If you see a comedian tell a joke on stage and then another comedian says the same joke, who do you lose respect for? The comedian that came second. Don't be the copycat comedian. You want to stay original and build a brand on what your company stands for. When you post your pictures and videos on social media, make sure you put your name on the image. You can also place a date on it. You are the originator.

Food is a gift and also art. Be creative in your art! Create dishes and displays that scream your brand. Only you can build it and the rest will come. Be honest and stay true to what you are creating. You won't need to mirror another company because you will build a brand off of how you want the world to recognize you.

Be Uniquely You!

Finally, building relationships with like-minded individuals who are on the similar path as you can help. Partnerships, collaborations, or just having a mentor can help with improving and growing in business. You can find persons you trust that will help with the challenges you may face along the way. Be willing to share content that may not be specific to your brand but generalized across the board for service. This can help everyone to know that there is a time for competition and also a time to help build one another. "Two heads are better that one!" is a very true statement. At least reach out to a trusted advisor, secure a mentor or be a mentor. It never hurts to reach someone that may be up and coming. I say there is enough for everyone to eat.

NOTES

NOTES

CHAPTER 8
BONUS CHAPTER

Pricing your product can be one of the hardest tasks you will have to do in business. In the food industry, you must stay competitive with the current food costs and your competitors... at least until you are established and have built a reputation that supersedes cost. In this final section, there are tools to help you create and design your costs specific to your company. Keep in mind all the costs you must include when creating your menu and pricing. Don't leave out anything, and remember, time is MONEY! No matter your industry, it is important to make money. Pricing your product accurately will help you to be successful in the long run. Your goal is to see green and stay out of the red when it comes to finances. I will teach you how to price your product with these simple guidelines that are easy to follow.

HOW TO PRICE YOUR PRODUCT!

Calculating your costs:
Actual Cost
Ideal Cost
We will discover how to accurately price your product with this simple cost analysis.

Actual Cost: Actual cost is the product's accurate price. It should include all expenses incurred in producing or delivering your product. This should include indirect costs such as your overhead, equipment, labor, delivery, and any other related costs.

Ideal Cost: Ideal cost is not an accurate calculation. It can vary depending on the type of food your serve and the overhead costs, as well as your operating expenses. An example of your operating expenses would be your rent, food costs, utilities, etc.

Before you determine the price of your company's meals, you must know how much they cost to make. You need to figure out how much it costs your restaurant or catering company to make one serving of each item on your menu.

Example:
Cost of a Chicken Sandwich…
1 Chicken Breast: $4
1 Brioche Bun: $.50
1tsp sauce: $.25
2 slices of cheese: $1
2 slices of tomato: $.75
1 serving of romaine lettuce: $.75
4+.50+.25+1+.75+.75=$7.25
Total cost of ingredients for the chicken sandwich would be $7.25
This is your cost to produce the item.

Now you can determine the final cost of your product a few different ways. One way is to determine your percentage and attach that percentage increase to each item sold. If your percentage increase is 30%, you take your cost of serving and multiply by 30%. Our chicken sandwich total cost would be $9.43. This is just an example. Average percentage mark up in restaurants and catering can range from 28%-35%.

How to determine your costs:
Overhead costs
Labor costs
Fixed costs
Allow for profit margin

Overhead costs:

• Figure out how much your overhead costs are per month. Your overhead is your utilities, advertising and marketing costs, and any other business-related costs that are not directly related to each working day or event. Once you determine this cost, you can charge a certain amount per event to cover your costs.

• Ex. If your rent is $1,000 per month, you have 10 events in that month, you should add an additional $100 per event to your final bill. You can disguise it as catering fees. The client does not need to know what the fee is for. Work it into your final invoice.

Labor costs:

• Calculate how much your labor fees are per day. Include prep time and delivery. In addition, you need to add staffing fees as well. The prep staff must be calculated in your price per person for your events or your restaurant menu pricing.

• Example: 5 hours/day, $18/hour with 4 staff members = $360

• If your event averages between 50-100 guests, break it down accordingly. $3.60 would be assessed per person in the overall fees of a party of 100. (These are only examples. You can adjust how you need.)

Determine Fixed Costs:

• Add the fixed costs and then multiply the per person charge by the number of guests. Add these numbers to get your final cost for the event and then add in your profit.

Allow for profit margin:

This can be flexible per event, depending on your client… if it's a large corporation or a small private event. Oftentimes it can be difficult, especially when you are just starting out. You can do it by a percentage or charge a fee. Its best to see what the client's budget is and try to work within their budget or your price is your price, and you stick to what you want your profit margin to be. (28%-35% is a range you can use for mark up.)

Another way to calculate your costs, which is much simpler, is using the standard up charge of 3 times or 3.5 times the cost.

Combine ALL of your costs of your food items that you will use. Take the total cost (COG-cost of goods) and multiply it by 3 or 3.5. Depending on the client, you can multiply as much as 5 times, especially during high demand periods to maximize profits during your company's busy season.

Example:
Cost of goods $2,000, multiply by 3.5 (my standard) =$7000 Divide by the amount of guests 200 guests = $35 pp
This is a sample of calculating, but make sure you include all the services. On top of this fee, you can add serving, labor, gratuity, service fee, delivery, set up, rentals, disposables, etc. Include ALL your costs!

When calculating your costs, you also must consider your labor fee. We often forget about ourselves and wait till after we've spent the money for supplies and goods to get "what's left". Don't cheat yourself. You, too, should get paid on the front end and the back end. Calculate your hourly costs in the labor fee as well for each event. At least set yourself a wage. If you come out on the lower end in the beginning, it's okay. You are building. $50 an hour to $250 an hour...determine your cost.

Once you determine your costs per serving, you can break down cost per event. To determine what you pay your staff, find out the average cost of prep and wait staff in your city. Make a profit per hour on each of your staff members and mark up what you pay at least $3-$5 to cover the costs of taxes and payroll. You have to match expenses from each check and make a profit on your end.

The minimum each staff is paid should be 4 hours. You also have to factor in set up and breakdown time.

Example:
Team arrives: 4 p.m.
Set up: 4-5 p.m.
Event begins at 5:30 p.m.-9:30 p.m.
Clean up: 9:30-10:30 p.m.

The fee I would charge a client would be 7-8 hrs. This will include my fee and give wiggle room for delays in set up.

You can also put the staff on a ranking in pay ranging from $15-$25 an hour. Still charge the client the highest rate per hour for each employee and profit the remainder unused funds for taxes and fees assessed.

These steps will help you in creating costs and budgeting for your company. You can structure according to your company's needs. The basic steps given will help determine your costs and to redesign your menu based on the cost analysis given.

SMILING SERVICE

NOTES

NOTES

On a Personal Note

I would like to thank you for trusting my experience and hope that my wisdom will help your business grow as it has mine. If you follow the guidelines I have laid out, watch the new path your company will begin to take. Make your company known for the service it provides, make the emails and references all positive. The ultimate goal is for someone to compliment you and your company when you are not in the room. Make your business known in your city for excellence. Word of mouth is powerful!

ROXANNE EASLEY

ABOUT THE AUTHOR

Roxanne Easley was born and raised in the inner city of Pittsburgh, Pennsylvania, called Homewood. Roxanne resides in the Pittsburgh area with her daughter, Tiara, where she is grooming her to be the next CEO of Roxanne's Catering.

Roxanne's Catering is established in Pittsburgh, PA, specializing in film catering, private event catering, corporate catering and more. Roxanne's Catering has been featured on screen in award award-winning films and television shows such as *Fences*; *American Rust*; *Mindhunter*; and *Manhunt*. Growing Roxanne's Catering for the last 18 years, she has seen the importance of service in the food industry. Roxanne has been established as a Culinary Professional since the age of 15. Although Roxanne is known for quality food, she is also well known for exceptional service.

Roxanne attended George Westinghouse High School, Edinboro University of Pennsylvania, and Penn Foster Career School. Discovering a love and passion for food at a very young age, she was inspired to make catering a lifetime career.

Roxanne's Catering's motto is, "You can have a great product, but people will not work with you if you have horrible service. A client can forgive a mistake, but that's only if you provide exceptional service!" Roxanne's belief is that service is more important than the product you are providing.

The reason behind that logic is your product can change and improve over time, but your service is what draws the customer to you and keeps them. The company has prided itself on excellent service and instilling the company's motto into other people's businesses. Roxanne presents a series of training courses to help entrepreneurs and their staff earn positive feedback on reviews for Google, Yelp or social media outlets. With this series, the ultimate goal is to increase sales. The key to a successful company is SERVICE… just look at, "Chick-fil-A"!

**For Smiling Service Training and other information,
Email:
SmilingServiceTraining@gmail.com**

www.ingramcontent.com/pod-product-compliance
Lightning Source LLC
Chambersburg PA
CBHW071203090426
42736CB00012B/2428